Make
Time to Pray

Isaiah 65:24

"And it shall come to pass, that before they call, I will answer; and while they are yet speaking, I will hear."

Parice C. Parker

Make Time to Pray

Copyright © 2016 by Parice Parker. All rights reserved.

Published by Fountain of Life Publisher's House
P. O. Box 922612, Norcross, GA 30010
Phone: 404-936-3989 Website: www.pariceparker.biz
Please Email Manuscripts to: publish@pariceparker.biz

Fountain of Life Publishing House is committed to excellence in the publishing industry. The Company reflects the philosophy established by the founder, based on Psalm 68:11, *"The Lord gave the word and great was the company of those who published it."*

Cover Design by Parice Parker
Editor: Dr. Nichol Burris Authored by: Parice C. Parker

Published in the United States of America
Copyright Library of Congress
ISBN: 978-1539382317
Date: November 28, 2017

DEDICATION

To all that need more prayer, those who want to understand the purpose of prayer, or for those who desire to know how to pray. *Make Time to Pray* will inspire you to pray while building a genuine prayer life with the Holy Spirit. There are powerful benefits you will inherit once you are made more aware of the effectual power of a powerhouse prayer warrior. Are you in need of answers, or looking to gain more spiritual knowledge to lead a more productive life along with attaining more abundant peace in your faith walk? *Make Time to Pray* is an essential, and very resourceful book that needs to be added to your daily library to enhance your communication skills with our Heavenly Father for you to inherit all you are destined to receive.

Parice C. Parker

DEFINITION OF *PRAYER*

1. A devout petition to God or an object of worship.

2. A spiritual communion with God or an object of worship, as in supplication, thanksgiving, adoration, or confession.

3. The act or practice of praying to God or an object of worship.

4. A formula or sequence of words used in or appointed for praying:

The Lord's prayer.

5. Prayers, a religious observance, either public or private, consisting wholly or mainly of prayer.

6. That which is prayed for.

7. A petition; entreaty.

CONTENTS

INTRODUCTION

So many people don't understand the purpose of prayer, and many think it's just a ritual or a tradition. There is so much power in prayer when it's effective. It is a way of communication to our Heavenly Father connecting to Him spiritually, and through our open discussion of exercising prayer. We can download anointing power that will add light to a dark place, give knowledge that will instruct wisdom to be evident in our lives, and replace curses for a blessing. Don't you want to live a more effective and productive life? Prayer will literally transform your life in a blink of an eye. It is definitely a life changer! We all need prayer, and with the power of prayer, your life will be transformed, but you must *Make Time to Pray.*

Praying is a necessity for all victories obtained and even in the greatest of failures. I realized through prayer, I was empowered to get back up, and run to see what my end would be. Life is not easy but it can be dazzling with goodness if you learn the power of prayer. If you need power in a hopeless situation just make time to pray. If you ever get in over your head, just *Make Time to Pray.* When you are really tired of losing out on life opportunities, just *Make Time to Pray.* In this book, *Make Time to Pray,* you will be enthused with generous supernatural power and your life conditions will be more peaceful, happy, and flowing with goodness while impacting lives to be inspired with a fresh ray of hope.

Prayer is your intimate time with The Holy Spirit and during this time you are able to communicate with God. Every strong relationship is fortified through good and healthy communication. Prayer is the God way and if you don't understand prayer you will not achieve real freedom in the things you are trying to accomplish. God will give you the Supernatural ability to accomplish even the impossible because with God, all things are possible. Prayer is the foundation of real movement and it will cause a good transformation. Prayer is the key that will unlock wisdom to be made manifest in your life and cause your faith to bring forth the evidence of what you are requesting of our Heavenly Father. Opening your prayer with the invocation, "Heavenly Father," is a form of submission and opens communication between you and God. This book will help you to *Make Time to Pray* and you will get better results in your prayer life.

Parice C. Parker

Chapter 1
Why Pray?

As I have learned, many people do not understand the power of having a genuine prayer life. Most have never been trained, been taught to pray, or even know how to pray? Some don't even know who they are praying to. As you continue on this journey with me, reading, *Make Time to Pray,* you will understand the dynamics of having a real prayer life and why you should never stop praying? It is imperative for you to understand prayer, and the importance of praying without ceasing. Prayer is your spiritual key to every "Yes" you will ever need, but you must make time to pray. Once you complete this book, please pass it along to someone that needs a more genuine prayer life because there is power in prayer. Prayer adds a sweet fragrance to your life, and it will draw goodness, mercy, favor, blessings and grace to you. Prayer builds our trust in the Lord so we can understand our purpose of being joint heirs unto His vision. After all, it is our Heavenly Father that created and invented over 192 nations, the lands, sea, skies, rivers, waters fall, damns, oceans, ponds, beaches, islands, stars, and named them one by one; plus countless more things. Also, each night He arranges and decorates the skies with impressive glimmering stars, hangs the moon up high in the sky, and in the morning He gently places the sun up high to brighten our day. He thought so much of us.! We serve a Mighty, Awesome God that is worthy to be praised, worthy to be gloried, and worthy to be trusted. He thought and thinks more of us than we think of ourselves. He is not selfish, and we shouldn't be either. Prayer simply keeps us connected to our Heavenly Father as we build a genuine relationship with Him. Each of us must earn our trust to stay committed. Quite naturally, God keeps His Word, but, all to often, we don't keep our commitments to Him. Prayer teaches us not to lean on our own understanding. He directs our path, even when we cannot see what is going on. I realize life will throw you many curve balls, and if you are not spiritually in tune, you will be caught off guard. So many people play Russian Roulette with their lives, not realizing the value of it.

"Trust in the LORD with all thine heart; and lean not unto thine own understanding."
Proverbs 3:5 (KJV)

Never try to understand the things that

would try to bring fear, doubt, or disbelief in your life. It is not worth it. There were many things for a long time that made no sense, and I needed explanations, but as time passed on, God revealed them to me. Now, going in I was clueless. See, this is a prime reason why you ought to always pray because in life many of things are just not going to make any sense, until later.

2 Chronicles 6:40

"Now, my God, let, I beseech thee, thine eyes be open, and let thine ears be attentive unto the prayer that is made in this place."

As we enter into prayer, it illuminates our spiritual eyes and gives us clearer insight regarding our life situations. Often in life, we don't have a clue of what we are going through, how to further life in the midst of traumatic situations, or how to maintain a safe and productive healthy life. But through the power of prayer, we are strengthened. Our ears must hear right direction and our minds must receive precise instructions, this happens when we *Make to Time Pray*. There is a place that our Heavenly Father must go, and that is in prayer. If it weren't for the power of prayer, I would not have made it this far; but because of it, I am still here. I will never forget this once a time I needed the power of God to move a mountain of sickness out of my way. There was not a doctor that had answers as to why I was going through this terrible time of illness, and I didn't feel I deserved. During this sick-bed of affliction, God spared my life. In 2007 a horrific moment changed the course of my life forever. One day, my family and I had just come home from dinner and everyone was laughing and joking as we entered the house. I was working on a manuscript that I was eager to finish. I ran upstairs to my office and began looking at the manuscript. My daughter had some homework to complete. She quietly asked me if she could use the computer sitting next to me. My children knew Mommy's office was off limits! But that particular day, I am grateful she was sitting right there. As I picked up my manuscript, an excruciating pain in my head began; my head was throbbing and the pain was unbearable. I told my daughter to call 9-1-1 and then to go get her dad. I struggled to make it to the den. I fell on the floor. I just knew I was going to die. I looked and saw my three children kneeling and praying for me. I thank God that at such a young age they were kneeling in a circle, touching and agreeing for my healing. That was the beginning of a door of great affliction I had to enter. As time passed, I grew sicker and sicker. Stroke after stroke, and my family truly suffered for many years afterwards as they endured the pain with me.

Matthew 18:19

"Again I say unto you, That if two of you shall agree on earth as touching anything that they shall ask, it shall be done for them of my Father which is in heaven."

I am so grateful my children knelt when I couldn't, and many days I wondered what if they hadn't? Prayer is precious; you should teach your children to pray and the importance of continual prayer. Now, just imagine if I was not a prayer warrior. I didn't know strokes were in my future, but many times I testified I was covered with the blood of Jesus going through my great affliction; many people have one stroke and die instantly. For years, afterward, I had many more strokes and the entire family was affected by my illness. See, my children honored *Matthew 18:19* and look at the results of that prayer. Prayer sustains life, upgrades over spiritual coverage, and causes God to move on our behalf because witnesses are observing His Miraculous Healing Power. He loves to receive GLORY. As my children locked hands in the Spirit, they united forces with our Heavenly Father for healing power for their myself. The Word is so powerful it will operate in your life in areas you cannot. That is the power of prayer and the incentives of the prayers of the righteous. Notice, the pure at heart can get a prayer to go up immediately, such as children, because their sins are not on them, but their parents. Also, their faith is stronger than most adults because children are more accessible to believing with a more profound imaginary mindset than we are able to comprehend. Most adults do not live by faith, they tend to go into prayer with doubt and little to no faith. A child will pray with complete belief in God that He will fix it; the majority of the adults will not. My children knew what to do in the time of need, and for that, I will never be able to thank God enough for such a memorable moment I will always CHERISH.

Chapter 2

Understanding the Purpose of Prayer

*C*hildren depend on their parents to take care of them. That is how God expects us to rely on Him. God wants us to be prepared for Him to take care of our needs. He is a jealous God, and He does not want us to put anything before Him, not even our loved ones. God wants us to glorify Him first; He also wants us to appreciate Him daily. For many years He has tended to the care of our families by ensuring us to wake up in the right state of mind. He has given us the ability to care for them. God wants our attention in and completely on Him. Can you imagine your child not paying you any attention for days, weeks, months, or years, especially, when they see you every day and live with you? Often, good parents have bent over backwards looking after their children and sacrificed dearly? God wants you to care about Him in this same manner. After all, you would not have made it this far without God.

Matthew 6:6 says,

"But thou, when thou prayest, enter into thy closet, and when thou hast shut the door, pray to thy Father which is in secret; and thy Father which seeth in secret shall reward thee openly."

Prayer can only surface through your heart, and God knows our hearts? That is why He needs to be positioned first in our life. When you come to God with a pure heart, everything will be set free in your life, and there will be no more secrets. Your life will be purposed to satisfy Him. God deserves better from us. He has a better plan for our life, this is why He gives us vision. He wants us to see we can have a better life, we must first kneel down in truth and begin to cast your cares on Him. Let God inspire you like never before. For the first time in your life, feel pure and know that your change has begun. It will be like no other prayer in your life; God delivered me, and He will do the same for you. When He moves you with The Anointing, every wrong thing will be served an eviction notice without warning, to get out of your life! Immediately, He put claims over your life, and the enemy will flee from your heart. You will never forget that prayer. It will be that special prayer which has caused your soul to be delivered and from that day forward, you will have a new start.

Psalm 105:15 Says,

"Touch not mine anointed, and do my prophets no harm."

God will touch you and put His Spirit of Calmness to live in you. If things in your life are troubled, hold on to His Word. You have extensive power in the inside of you that is not yet speaking of your life. God is a God who fully rewards His children of obedience, and He remembers the way we bless Him in secret. He gives us our heart's desires. God offers us the liberty to make our own choices. Nothing can stop or hold God back from working powerfully in your life, but you. Satan does not have the power over your future if God is in control of your life? All you have to do is kneel down in prayer with an expectancy to be delivered. Open your heart and watch God fulfill you. Though some things may later try you, God will not let it touch you. His covering will speak to the enemy, "Touch not my Anointed, and do my Prophet no harm."

Bow when you are in need, speak to God with your heart and tell Him you desire to love Him. He will teach you how to love Him; satisfy Him, and He will satisfy you. *Psalm 90:14 says, "O Satisfy us early with thy mercy; that we may rejoice and be glad all our days."* Listen to God as He speaks to you and allow Him to lead you into His presence. God loves you and He will satisfy all your heart's desires. God tells us through His Word that He will give us our heart's desires. When we seek Him, every need will be given to us and every prayer will be answered. Just imagine how important that day will be, not just for your life, but also for everyone that is exposed to you. That is Anointing Power! God will make you glad. He will change your life in a manner that you will begin to rejoice every day in Him.

1 Thessalonians 5:17,

"Pray without ceasing."

As you begin to pray, there is no need to stop. Every time you stop, the enemy forces himself into your life. Through the years I, too, have begun praying, and somewhere along the way I stopped. I had to start all over again from square one. Developing a prayer life takes time, and it is not going to happen in the blink of an eye. An effectual prayer life develops through our prayer experiences. It takes time to build a never-failing faith. God's timing is different from ours and His pace is at a supernatural flow.

2 Peter 3:8

"But, beloved, be not ignorant of this one thing, that one day *is* with the Lord as a thousand years, and a thousand years as one day."

23

If God stops being God for a day, tell me, how would He supply us mercy in the time of our need? Look around at the hospitals; millions are on life support daily throughout the world. They are living not because of life support, but by prayer support. Perhaps, they are residing abroad through their prayers of co-workers, church members, friends, family and, even sometimes, the prayers of strangers. Many people will join forces together to pray at such a needed time, and God is going to answer someone's prayer. You never know whose prayers God is answering first. I do not know many people who would pleasantly open up their front door to a stranger, even after properly introducing themselves. Well, that is how God is to us daily. He opens up His windows of Heaven to look out and see just whom it is calling upon His name. Also, if it is an unfamiliar voice, then there is much proof you will need for God to open up. Just for myself, it has taken years to receive my prayer power. Just as David stayed in touch with God, we, too, must keep our relationship with God. I have endured many hours of tears, prayers, church settings, worship times, Holy Communion, and study-time in the Word just to reach this point in my life. I have worked hard for God to get to know who I am. You must continually prepare by folding your hands in prayer and never stop the Spirit of God from moving in your life. I cannot count the prayers, days, and nights that I was lifted up or the tears that rolled down my cheeks. No matter what comes your way, just continue to pray. Yes, many things are going to try you, but keep on praying. The enemy works for the purpose of keeping us away from God. Do not give into any more excuses and do not let him keep you away from God. Remember, it is imperative that you *Make Time to Pray.*

Psalm 91:1

"He that dwelleth in the secret place of the Most High shall abide under the shadow of the Almighty."

Chapter 3
Take the Opportunity to Pray

*J*esus gave me the opportunity to be a part of the tree of life, and I am forever grateful unto God for that opportunity. If you have ever taken notice of the tree of life, some branches are connected, and to every branch there's hope, love, faith, guidance, rewards, heavenly things, favor, Power from on High, due inheritance, and Anointing Power. Also, you will receive life eternal, blessings, assurance, increase, prosperity, good things, healing, miracles, and everything that is dead is ultimately brought to life. An opportunity is not something that is forced on you. It is something that only you can recognize it's real value and appreciate its worth by accepting it with an immense gratitude within your heart. His presence will shadow your ground and cover you always.

Opportunity

1) An appropriate or favorable time or occasion:

Their meeting afforded an opportunity to exchange views.

2. A situation or condition favorable for attainment of a goal.

3. A good position, chance, or prospect, as for advancement or success.

1 Thessalonians 5:19 says,

"Quench not the Spirit."

A tree is something that begins with a seed, and as that seed is cultivated it eventually produces life as a result. Nevertheless, a tree does not grow over night. The seed must be planted first, just like our prayer life. The more we begin to pray, the more we begin to develop. The more one is rightfully developed, they can gain more access with their maturity, such as investment funds. The more you invest in a safe marketing account, the more your investment can increase your benefits. Our prayer life is the same. The more we pray with a pure heart, the more we establish a good and healthy standard of communication with God. Also, the more we hear Him and obey His voice, the more access we gain to daily self-improvement. Opportunities offer a chance for prosperity, accessing you the ability to increase and be strengthened in God. Every time you stop praying, you allow the enemy to come and rearrange your life. You need *The Anointing*; you must continue to pray without ceasing. Each time you stop praying puts a halt and hold on The Anointing to flow in your life. You have an opportunity to receive the power of God by folding your hands in prayer and bowing your head. We all have the chance to fold our hands in prayer and to gain power from on High. In most cases, many people give the enemy power over their prayer life by not praying. Let God shadow your life. Satan knows when we are not covered. A faithless prayer life intoxicates the blessed life that God wants for you. When people walk in stumbling conditions, it is an embarrassment, and it's not showing that God lives in them. However, it does demonstrate to the world that you are off balance, unstable, and you are walking without the power of God in your life. God wants to shadow your life. Get covering in prayer.

Psalm 91:4 says,

"He shall cover thee with his feathers, and under his wings shalt thou trust: his truth shall be thy shield and buckler."

Every second within an hour someone needs God's attention, and that is how busy He is. Can you imagine every emergency that's going on at one time throughout the entire world? God does not have time to sleep, rest, nor slumber. He is a very attentive and watchful God. He is always taking care of His children's needs by being a God with grave concern. Do not leave home without prayer. Treat your prayer life as if it is your insurance policy. Make sure you are covered. Troubles are always waiting to occur and you do not want to encounter difficulty without being fully covered. David was one that was covered by God; he was under the shadow of The

Wings of God. He took the time to get to know God, and that is why he was always covered. When he fell, He was covered. As he stumbled, and as he battled, God covered him. Make sure you are covered through your day as you leave home, and before you lay to rest at night. However, the more you pray, your insurance policy increases with Him. The more you pray, it upgrades your trust in Him. Satisfy God with your prayer and watch how He will soon give you the desires of your heart.

1 Thessalonians 5:18

"In everything give thanks: for this is the will of God in Christ Jesus concerning you."

I love how David would not allow sin to stop him from proving his love to God. Too many people allow their sinful nature to allow guilt to rest heavy in their heart and they quit praying. Also, many people give Satan the opportunity to persuade them to lower their standards; then they quit praying or slow down their praying power. Eventually, sin will overtake your confidence in God and swap it out for doubt, fear, and make you scared to bow down. Satan knows his game, but you must overcome all his tricks. No matter what David did, he continued to worship, pray, and praise God. The Book of Psalm in the Bible consist of writings such as: Poems, Poetry, Prayers, Songs, and Love stories David wrote to minister to God. He constantly tried to prove his love for God though he slipped and fell numerous times. He would not quit trying to please God, and he always repented.

One thing you must understand: God loves you. Jesus suffered too much for you to take this opportunity of life for granted. Never take your prayer life for granted, and never let the enemy scare you. Jesus' whole life, as He walked the face of this earth, was to prove His love, first to His Father; secondly to you, and thirdly to the enemy. Every work He did, He uplifted, exalted, and glorified His Father. Jesus is the prime example that you can overcome, and you can conquer the enemy with power, but you must stay prayed up. Jesus intended for us to pray as He did. He took the time to teach us how to pray. All along, He was showing us how to honor His Heavenly Father. Jesus separated Himself from others in order to pray; He was teaching us how to follow His example. Jesus took His prayer life seriously because He was guiding us to His Heavenly Father. He is the guide to Heaven. You need guidance; if you do not take the time to pray, then you will never receive it. God has a perfect plan, specifically for you to live, and God wants to promote your lifestyle. He wants others to see how He blesses those that are obedient to His Word. There are so many people watching and waiting for you to make it; they are noticing how God is working miracles out for you. Our life speaks for itself, but is it truly speaking that God lives. God wants you to obtain a supernatural lifestyle that is going to cause many people to kneel down in prayer. You must pray because your power to overcome is in the way you kneel down, and reverence God during your prayer. Things may not appear to be going in the manner you would have wanted them, but continue being thankful. God wants us to appreciate everything in life, including our trials and tribulations. God is in full control of our lives.

Through the years, I've learned to thank God for everything. It's a beautiful thing, even during your hard times, that you can still thank God from the depths of your heart just for being God, in and over your life.

Matthew 6:7 says,

"But when you pray, use not vain repetitions, as the heathen do: for they think that they shall be heard for their much speaking."

Just imagine being given a certain task to perform, but you never considered the instructions given or think of following through. Instructions are necessary, and a reward is at the end of each completed task. Surely, you want good things to happen in your life, but are you prepared to do what is needed for you to achieve it? There is a time in your life for everything, and now is the time for a real serious prayer life. As you begin to care about your prayer life and the seriousness it has over your life, then God will begin to take good care of your prayers. Once you become deeply concerned with the responsibilities of being a prayer warrior, then God gets concerned about blessing your life and answering your prayers. So, therefore, at no time can God afford His time to be wasted. God's time is valuable! There is someone else receiving His full attention through their prayers. God wants you to pray in truth, not being concerned about big revolving words, but merely just opening up your heart to Him. God does not need another person to pray aloud so that others can hear; God needs a prayer warrior that is ready and willing to fulfill His desires. Many preachers love to pray openly on the roster, but many of them also pray without power. What good is it to pray one day out of the week just because people are going to hear you, and you have not knelt down on your knees to pray all week long? God knows us through our secret closet and He knows every time we pray unto Him with sincerity from our hearts.

Chapter 4

Add Power to Your Prayer Life

*F*or anything to grow, it takes time. If you want real praying power, then you need to give it time. If you do not sow the seed of prayer, how can you expect to gain the power in your prayer? Regardless of whatever you want to grow in your life, you must *Make Time to Pray*. Growing is a process; it just takes time. Over a period of time, God will enrich your praying power. I often say, "If you want something done, you must do it yourself." If you want God to hear you, then you need to begin speaking to God for yourself, kneeling and bowing down, continuously, in prayer reverencing The Almighty Father. I have learned over the years that sometimes we can exhaust ourselves in prayer, and it is due to insufficient praying power. How can you pray without electricity? It takes power to surge anything, it takes the power of electricity to turn on the lights. Surely, you can flick the switch on, but if the power is disconnected, the lights still won't turn on. If you put your car key in the ignition, and turn the key switch and find the battery is dead, you know it won't start unless you get a boost or a jump start? Or, if you are out of gas, the care might start, but it won't go anywhere. Without everything being properly prepared, it's powerless. One powerless thing will stop power from surging to other vital parts for effective operation.

II Corinthians 5:7 says,
"For we walk by faith, not by sight:..."

God wants you to be motivated, not through your sight, but by your faith. Encouraged, not through your sight, but by your faith.

He wants you to be fully prepared at all available times in order to receive all that He has for you. He wants you to keep your mind stayed on the finished work, not the beginning of the work or even care about the trying times of the work that He has given you. He doesn't want you to focus on your ability, your strength, nor your capabilities. Focus on His Power surging through you as you earnestly pray. For many years, I, too, prayed, but I prayed powerlessly. A powerless prayer will exhaust your life because it's hard without seeing change. If you want your life to change, then your prayer must change from powerless to The Anointing. In addition, God has all of the Anointing Power you will ever need, just put your hands on it. Get thirsty in your soul for The Anointing to overtake you. To start anything, particularly, with an anointed prayer life, you need power from on High. A certain essence gets the power surging in your prayer life. God yearns for a true prayer warrior, and Jesus was one of the best. I can imagine He summed it all up in the model prayer of teaching us how to pray. Still, I fully believe that He knew; He had faith that God had already taken care of His needs. So, therefore, most of His prayers were for other peoples' needs. Jesus never had a selfish heart when He prayed. Therefore, as you pray, your heart must be clear to hear God as a selfish heart will never reach God's heart.

James 5:16

"Confess your faults one to another, and pray one for another, and that ye may be healed. The effectual fervent prayer availeth much."

You never know when you are going to need a dying emergency from God. It is so valuable to stay prayed up with His Anointing Power because it's truly up to you how much you are willing to value your prayer life with God. There is no sense of praying and you have no power. In order to receive power from God you must first crank it up. How can a car start without the key in the ignition just an example, you cannot hot-wire a prayer? The key to cranking up your prayer life is to kneel down in the correct way to God. As you begin to kneel, you must be prepared to kneel down with an open heart, readily to confess your wrongs. In every case, the addict will not admit their faults in the beginning, until the addiction has overtaken them. For so long the enemy has entrapped our minds, hearts, bodies and souls because we are not honest enough to confess our faults. Most people are too busy pinpointing other peoples' mistakes. Wrong is wrong, and right is right. It's just like walking into a situation blindfolded. If so many would have knelt down to pray before they began their day, then so many would not have experienced that demon addiction, doing something crazy, getting arrested, raping someone, and the list can go on. You never know what the end of your day will bring that will forever change your life. Many people wish they had another opportunity to go back in time to change what they had done wrong. He wants you to get a new mindset, and that is to keep your mind on Him!

Matthew 26:41 says,

"Watch and pray, that ye enter not into temptation: the spirit is willing, but the flesh is weak."

That is why it is so valuable for us to not

stop praying because we must tune into the Spirit of God first thing in the morning as we begin to open our eyes. Whether it's day or night that you wake up, it's time to pray. Do you ever think to pray to God not to lead you into temptation? Just imagine, what if 50% of every human being is truly guilty of their crimes and sitting in prison or on death row had prayed this prayer alone? Every evil temptation that is upon the face of this earth is a tempting spirit of the enemy to attack our spiritual development, happiness, good health, wealth, and prosperity. God is a God of assurance, love, results, deliverance, freedom, hope, peace, and joy. All of these equal the good that will develop out of your spiritual life through the power of prayer. As you begin to paying attention, you will start to notice that nothing can go forward in your life without the power of God authorizing it and allowing it. Many of us get to a certain point where we just can't bare life, and we realize we want more. But in wanting more, you can only get it through God. Now you are prepared to expect a difference to receive what you are seeking out of this life. Prayer is the key to opening up God's heart to flow into your life. I began praying like never before in the year of 1999 and as I prayed this particular night, I did not give it any thought. I just knelt down, but as I began doing so, I knew God was going to hear my supplication. I went to God like never before, feeling a profound urgency, and I needed immediate attention. The way my heart felt this night was like no other night I had yet experienced. I longed for God in a manner of confessing my wrongs, and all I wanted was for God to make me right. I went down expressing everything from the inside out. I began pouring out my heart. When I knelt down it was nightfall, but when I rose up the birds were singing, and the sun had risen. This night of prayer was the most beautiful night I ever had. As I knelt down, I was feeling weak and needy, but when I rose up, I rose in His glorious power. I do not remember everything, but I know that God was all in it. I believe He answered every single need for the rest of my life just through this one prayer because God felt my heart. I did not kneel down in doubt, but I knelt down in genuine fear for my life, soul, and family - I knelt down in faith. I knew what I was, but I also knew that only God could change me. This prayer was my life changing prayer; God wants to change your life from being powerless to becoming all powerful. He intends to anoint the work of your hands, and He even wants to give you the greater works. This one scripture I asked God for *Proverbs 14:27, "The Fear of the Lord is a fountain of life to depart from the snares of death."* And through that request, over the years, God granted me just what I asked for: a Fountain of Life. I am also the CEO of Fountain of Life Publisher's House and Fountain of Life Empowerment. These are evidence that my prayer was powerful and effective that night. It was so powerful in the Spirit, Fountain of Life Publisher's House was conceived immediately.

James 5:15 says,

"And the prayer of faith shall save the sick, and the Lord shall raise them up; and if he has committed sins, they shall be forgiven him."

You must begin something new that you never had in your prayer life in order to get God's attention immediately. The Spirit of

God is so willing to change your life. As long as there is a will of God, surely, there is a way. You must not trust yourself (flesh), because you are weak, and you will fall if God is not in it. Even Jesus had to kneel, and He is powerful, but He never stopped kneeling to receive His power. Everything Jesus did was because He wanted His Father's heart to be happy. You must have the same willingness to pray in order for God to will His Spirit in the time of your need. Jesus never looked through fleshly eyesight because He was always seeing through His spiritual eyes. Jesus allowed the Spirit of God to feed His Spirit daily. Think of it as the vehicle you drive. As your driving around the city, your gas begins to run low, sooner than later, you will need to fill up again. I always think of my prayer life that way because it's a hurting feeling when you run out of gas and I don't ever want to run out of power from on High. You never know what situation you might encounter that you will need the power of your prayer to get you or someone else out of a situation immediately. I pray earnestly because as God fills me and as I go on I need more of Him. As you continue your new prayer life, the enemy is going to try to grow larger and stronger in your life because he wants to stop you from praying as an attempt to weaken your faith. But, remember God is greater than all the enemy. The enemy loves to try to throw you off balance and catch you off guard. One thing you must understand, the more you grow spiritually, the stronger you'll become. If you have the power of God completely on your side, the enemy can't touch you because The Most High, and All-Powerful God is guarding your life and the enemy cannot overpower God. Therefore, God needs to be in full control of your life and not you.

Luke 11:20 says

"When a strong man armed keepeth his palace, his goods are in peace."

As you continue to pray for power, your covering, which is our Heavenly Father, begins to shield and protect you. However, as I continued through an almost seemingly impossible fight, I realized that I started fighting for a more fervent prayer life. I got so tired of people's excuses. One of my favorite ones is, "I have to work." For so long, I told people, "The reason you are working two jobs is because you need strength from the Lord. I have never seen the righteous forsaken, forgotten, nor left behind." Living life for self will cause forces from the enemy to seclude your mind, praise, prayer life, worship, and the gathering of Saints. If God has blessed your life and if you keep on your Armor of His Spirit, you will never have to worry about the enemy tearing down your house.

I will never forget a sermon my husband preached, "*How Bad Do You Want It?*" Man, did I grasp it? Being a Christian is one thing, but it's an entirely different aspect being a powerful weapon. There was a time when our oldest son needed to move in with us, and I believe he thought I was crazy. There were certain things that I just would not allow to go on in our household. God wants you to stay protected through His Spirit and keep daily watch over the things that we allow into our homes. A True Believer that is of great power for God must stand their ground, even when they can't see it, they still must stand because of the power of their faith. You cannot allow any and everything in the world to be in your home. I am very prayerful in my home, over my home, and even after someone leaves my home. I believe in the power of prayer, and it is stronger to me than I know my first and last name. I had to come to realize in my life that absolutely nothing will separate me from the love of God; no excuse is allowing to come out of my mouth. No reason is good enough to give God, and no one is greater to me than He is; therefore, I love expressing my devotion to Him. I believe when you begin to care about your prayer life, then you will start to care about God.

No, we didn't have to take that church in its condition, but I prayed and asked God for an area that needed us and if that is the building that God blessed us with then I was thankful, and so were some of the congregation. We must understand how precious our gratitude is to God because He said if we can be faithful over a few, then He would add all things unto us. In that broken state of a building was God's fortifying plan for our ministry growth, development, and our hearts began growing more spiritually. Within these bare walls and leaking roof, God supplied us generous mercy because we appreciated what He had blessed us with. The power of prayer was able to surge greater power within our lives through the Fountain that begins replenishing our lives with power. Within this messed up building was the impressive presence of the Lord. He awakened something on the inside of me that I thought I already had. He gave me the heart to yearn for the righteousness in others that were walking on the outside of the building. There were many prostitutes, drug addicts, children fallen by the wayside, and this community was a laughing joke to many. God blessed my heart to feel their need to want change so that many others can see their beauty through the power of God. I knew this job was greater than my husband and I put together. My husband, who is our Honorable Bishop, I love so dearly for believing in the power of God. He never gave up on our ministry, neither did He give up on me! This job needed the anointing of God to overflow and spread abroad. So, I had to begin a deeper prayer journey. No matter how good you begin to pray, you will always need to take a deeper plunge in the Spirit of God in your prayer life. The passion that God has given me to help others was great and mighty.

Make Time to Pray

John 17:9

"I pray for them: I pray not for the world, but for them which thou hast given me; for they are thine."

While many walked out of this ministry because of our workload, the needed amount of finances to operate this massive mission and the unity that had to be enforced, they missed something that money just could not buy. Instead of you putting your eyes on the amount of creativity of your mission; the hardship that it is going to take to make this all possible, just remember that God moves in every impossible situation. No matter what our circumstance was, I believed God for the greater. I never looked at our needs and thought that God could not do it. I realized, here in this mess of a building, God needed to gain something from me that I just did not have. Many of our members missed out on their faith inheritance and spiritual development because God never wanted us to feel the pressure of getting this building done. He wanted us to see how so many souls have been undone spiritually. This opportunity was one of the deeper faith unities that God had ever embarked on the Fountain of Life Christian Ministries and my personal life. Sometimes, God will try your heart just to see where you stand. Even though He already knows you, He just wants to show you something that is going to add greatness through His Spirit to strengthen you with pure, robust faith. As you look on the things of your life that seem impossible, I am here to tell you that it is all possible. I do not care how bad it is, just remember, "How bad you want it?" If God gave it to you then it is already yours, stop letting the things of this world get you down and allow the power of God to lift you up. Put your hands on whatever it is that God said for you to do and never focus on the impossibilities of your vision, but keep your mind focused on how God can make it all possible just for you. *Luke 14:18 says, "And they all with one consent began to make an excuse. The first said unto him, I have bought a piece of ground, and I must say needs go and see it: I pray thee have excused me."*

Luke 14:19 says,

"And another said, I have married a wife, and therefore I cannot come."

I grew through all the excuses people can give you when you need then, and I am still growing. Often, I just break out in praise because I know, and when you know something, nobody can change your mind. I thank God for His Son all the time because

Jesus has truly been my role model. When you realize the power that your prayers hold, peace will begin to surround everything within your life, regardless of how bad things will sometimes get. You must not focus on the bad things in your situations, but you have to focus on your victory through the power of prayer. God does not want to hear our excuses or bickering complaints. Excuses just disappoint the occasion, the moments that are special, and oppress relationships. Do you remember how you felt when people gave you excuses? So, why give God an excuse for being too busy to pray? He just wants you to believe that He Is. He knows within your heart that He is God. Never put anything before God. He is waiting for you to open up your heart so He can expand His Anointing Power in you.

Chapter 5

Add Ammunition to Your Prayer & Make a Powerful Impression

On this day, you will understand the power of having a genuine prayer life. We deal with natural and unnatural forces daily that are purposed to destroy us. So many people are lost in this world because they have no true spiritual adviser. It is important to have spiritual parents or loved ones that will show you how to pray. Many people have never been introduced to having such a prayer life. Demons are not kind; neither do they have a conscious to care. So many people are possessed and don't even know it, their family members are under terrible attacks, and no one notices because they are blind in the Spirit. If you do not know the operations of demonic forces, you will continue to ignore the fact that they are looking you right in your face. Demons love filth, mess, and darkness. There is nothing nice, clean, or peaceful when dealing with demons. Noticeably, demons never travel alone. This fact is the reason why one needs a dedicated prayer life which will manifest a yoke destroying anointing. Once the Holy Ghost comes upon you, you can accomplish anything and those demons must flee. You are going to have to make a definite choice if you want a better life. Decipher between the two, do I want the Anointing, or do I want this sinful thing? Whether it's a relationship, an addiction, or an assignment that you sat down on, the anointing is your exterminating power to destroy the demons that are assigned to stop you. Demonic forces are commissioned to attack our lives in every angle from health, wealth, prosperity, and our spirituality. Demons are very real, and their mission is to make life unbearable for you to live. *These evil forces want you to turn away from God in order for Satan to become the master your life. His main purpose is to kill, steal, and destroy your hope (John 10:10).* Where there is no hope, faith cannot grow. In life, you need faith to accomplish anything because faith is what strengthens the believer's will power.

Proverbs 3:5 says,

"Trust in the Lord with all thine heart; and lean not unto thine own understanding."

I would have never made it this far having all those strokes, but due to my faith and belief in praying power, I was healed. It is imperative to have a high-performance prayer life, especially, when issues are tormenting you trying to disable your trust in God. Life issues can cause one to be hopeless and live carelessly. The Word of God is like a machine gun, and it will kill and destroy every wicked, evil force that's trying to kill you. I remember I preached a message, "Where Is Your Ammunition?" So many people fail to realize everyday life is a battle field. So, you better prepare yourself to not be executed. I know the word executed seems harsh, but it's true. Look at how many different demons are waiting to assault your mind, ready to destroy your family's impression of you, and steal the joy out of your love ones at home. I have learned to go into a prayer closet and pray my strength because as you empty yourself out spiritually to our Heavenly Father, He will strengthen you to handle the battle.

Remember, this battle is not yours; It's the Lord's.

Matthew 6:6 says,

"But thou, when thou prayest, enter into thy closet, and when thou hast shut the door, pray to thy Father which is in secret; and thy Father which seeth in secret shall reward thee openly."

This time is not to be taken for granted because He needs you to make a great definition in life, to impact others. People around you will be able to feel and see the Power of the Lord upon you. It is through that power that people will be saved, healed, restored, and delivered. No longer shall you just wound your enemies, but through your praying power our Heavenly Father will give you heavenly ammunition. You will impact lives and make ever lasting impressions, even on the wicked forces that flee. You have been bullied long enough! Your family and friends will recognize the Holy Ghost ammunition provided by none other than God, The Father, for your victories. They will see your strength' strength obtained through praying power. Who would have thought when you *Make Time to Pray* one could receive divine revelation, knowledge, wisdom, and power? What you don't know, can hurt you!

Chapter 6

Infusion

Matthew 6:6 says,

"But thou, when thou prayest, enter into thy closet, and when thou hast shut the door, pray to thy Father which is in secret; and thy Father which seeth in secret shall reward thee openly."

*I*t's a designated place, naturally and spiritually, in which you must go in order for you to activate your prayer life. When you enter, shut the door! Once the door has been shut, no one can enter unless you open the door and invite them in. This is a very private and secular time between you and the Holy Spirit. No One Should Be Permitted Access.! It's a quiet place where you can make your petitions known; as the Holy Spirit will be awaiting your arrival. Too many people leave their door open anticipating interruptions. Awe, that is so rude!

Make your prayer time private and intimate with the Holy Spirit. He loves meeting in secret places so He can bless you wide openly. Set your prayer time(s) aside from your daily schedule and keep your infusion appointments. It's just like getting gas when you see the fuel light come on in your vehicle. Oftentimes, we are so busy we run out of gas on the way to our destination. If you never fill up, eventually, you will break down somewhere in life. Some people break down in very dangerous places, such as a high crime area and the thieves are right there waiting for your arrival to strip you of your valuables. This is a prime example of why you need to recheck your power sources regularly. Make sure you don't run out of pushing power for your life because it can cause you to go through some dangers that weren't meant for your life. And, when those times occur we put everyone else in jeopardy. I will give you an example in a few minutes as you read on.

Infuse means to implant and impart something in you. *Make Time to Pray* is purposed to impregnate you with vision and to help reboot your charge so you can become more than a conqueror. The longer we live, we will learn and listen to life lessons because they will speak to you. Our day to day life activities will cause us to feel the pressures of life that have the power to overwhelm us. When we are overwhelmed, we are not motivated to pray. Lack of prayer can cause lack of clarity. Lack of clarity can cause us to head down a path or paths not meant for us to travel. *Make Time to Pray will* lead you in the right direction, and send out warning signals to stop you from going down the wrong path in life. Do you remember the story about Jonah?

Jonah 3:3, says,

"Now the WORD of the LORD came to Jonah the second time, saying, 3) ARISE, go to Nineveh, that great city, and preach to it the message that I tell you."

You want to be in a position to be able to hear God and follow His instructions. Yes, God will speak to us and give us instructions in order for His plan to operate smoother. We are the partakers of Gods vision and plan. Jonah begins on his journey to preach, and took a detour caused by fear rather than faith. He got a second chance and he didn't want to disobey God's instructions again because he knew cursed circumstances would follow if he did.

Jonah 1:1-2, says,

"NOW the WORD of the Lord came to Jonah the son of Amittai. ARISE, go to Nineveh, that great city, and cry out against it; for their wickedness has come up before Me."

God had given Jonah an assignment to preach deliverance to a very wicked city, they were doing everything possible to displease God; they had absolutely no respect for Him. One will never get good results out of dishonor. Perhaps, Jonah was afraid because he felt no one would listen to him. It seems he entered the city alone and he didn't have anyone supporting him on this journey. Yes, it's a lonely place being a preacher, but when you have been called to an assignment, you must overcome every challenging thing.

Jonah 1:3, says,

"But Jonah arose to flee to Tarshish; so he paid the

fare, and went down into it, to go with them to Tarshish from the presence of the Lord."

Instead, Jonah went the opposite direction of His God given instruction. He fled to Tarshish, and he paid the fare. We will end up paying too much for disobedience.

Chapter 7

Prayer Is A Faith Increaser

Proverbs 3:5, says,

"Trust in the Lord with all thine heart; and lean not unto thine own understanding."

God has spoken to you and He has given you a commission. Perhaps, more than once, you have heard His voice; now it is time to listen. Moreover, you heard Him as He whispered to you. Many times, you have dreamed of your life being everything you ever hoped for, then you woke up, still stuck in your life. Often saying, "What if this dream was true?" and yet, still hoping that you could live that exact dream; sometimes feeling you would be better off if you had never awakened. Surely, we all have felt that way one time or another, especially, when we cannot handle the pressures of life. Many things have appeared in our lives that we did not expect. Life crisis has thrown you off guard and the way your life appears was nowhere in your life plans. Things happened to you without notice and many times, you wished your life were the dream that you had been dreaming. *It seems as though many of us have been marked to be destroyed.* Moreover, none of this was supposed to happen to you, but it did. Nevertheless, still no real proof of your dreams coming to reality due to a person's faith being weak. Perhaps, you have tried, and you may have tried in many ways. Still nothing seems to have worked out. You want a better life, but how bad do you desire it? Your hopes soon turn to dreams and your dreams soon turned into a brief moment of happiness, until you wake up. Sometimes, your mind has drifted into your dream world hoping for the dream to come true. Moreover, doubt begins to laugh in your face and surfaces in your mind, now your dreams are canceled out. Your hopes are now hopeless and there is no desperation causing you to continue to hope for your dreams to come true. However, you wanted it all to happen; growing up with many great expectations for your life, but your life has seemed to go down the drain. I am here to tell you that you need this vision to work, do not quit hoping for it now! Find yourself a new hope and let your new hope cause your dreams to come true. If God did it for me, He too can do it for you. The key is no matter what happened in my life, I never stopped dreaming. I never gave up and I was not prepared to let anything stop me. Slam on the gas and get off the brakes, let your dreams accelerate. You need it to be real! Let your effort push you forward. Your life destiny is depending on it. You want it and you have tried in every way, but did you give it all you had? Did you push yourself into God's Anointing Power? When you reach the depths of His power, your vision will speak boldly. His Anointing will prosper your vision. Increase will flow into operation. I want you to understand this one thing: only you can cause it to come forth. If you do not desire it strong enough then God does not have to let it happen. Perhaps your dreams were not large enough to cause Him to move on your behalf. However, He intentionally wanted you to believe in Him for a miracle that is going to forever affect the way you think of Him. Dreams are in a world of its own, but reality is what you live in. Let God bring your dreams into reality. No matter how large your dreams are, remember, God will give you your heart's desires. If you desire it, then it is yours! If you believe that He is able, then it is already done! If you know Him, then what are you still doing dreaming? God is a God of prosperity and He lives to purposely cause the dead to rise in Him. Get more God! All you have to do is delight yourself in Him.

Psalm 37:4 says,

"Delight thyself also in the Lord, and he shall give thee the desires of thine heart."

Just think about all the things you will be able to do with the Anointing Power of God working in your hands. If you use what He has blessed you with, you will receive The Anointing. You will have the power to do anything you set your mind to do. It does not matter how big your dreams are. God has the power to bring them all to reality. It does not matter if you have multiple visions. I mean enough to fill the largest football stadium in the world. It can happen for you. It does not matter if your dreams are great enough to fill a whole city or even the world. This is an example of how large God wants your heart's desire to be in Him. Your dreams will only live through the faith that you have in The Power of God. If you think small, you will only believe a little in Him. Get over that mustard seed of faith and let your faith grow up in Him. God wants to develop your faith, as He will cause it to mature. Allow Him to manifest everything within your life. Let Him give you the kind of hope that will cause you to gain more life. As you gain a greater life, many others will survive off of your hope. It is time to realize the depth of your faith receiving many life opportunities that will come to fruition just because of your dreams. God has the power for you to do it all. How many lives can be affected through the reality of your dreams? The work of your hands is going to affect many to be encouraged in Him or discouraged. Your hands possess power, but which power do they currently possess? Are they affecting lives to desire Him more or are they canceling out someone else's faith? Sometimes our dreams do not come true because God is not finished showing us the whole dream. Other times, it is because our hearts are not finished growing in Him. He wants The Power of Love to work through our hands. He wants someone else to be connected to Him through our works. He wants our lives to speak that He is real and to know that He lives. You need spiritual motivation; it is the only possibility for you to achieve all the visions He has given you. The Anointing can do it all. It is just waiting on you. I am one that knows about vision. I, too, have had many. I have had so many that someone once said, "Do you think you are trying to do too much at one time?" At first, I thought I did, but it was my many dreams that kept me running forward. Apparently, I was, but I believed so much in the Word of God and I knew He gave them all to me so I was not prepared to put one vision on the back burner. Soon afterwards, Jamie Fox appeared on The Oprah Show - a very gifted man in many ways. He said, "You can do it all!" Looking back over his many accomplishments, I realized if he could, then so could I. He is one with many talents and has been a great achiever in many ways. Remember, if someone else can, then so can you. Although you might think your dreams are too big, they are just right for God to bless them to come forth.

Every vision that God has given you is for a purpose. He wants you to put your hands on it. My visions helped saved my life. I simply needed them all. I began to work in every angle I could in order to achieve. They all lifted my spirits and kept me motivated in Him. Many times, I wanted to give up, but I could not. When God gives you a vision, it is made to be spiritual. His Spirit saved my life repeatedly and the many visions caused me to run on. Every song, book, business, and vision for the ministry was God's way of giving me hope. God wants you to hold on and move forward in your life. Things will get better. Actually, they will be so good at times that you will begin to burst out and just laugh. God has a mighty way of making us laugh without anything being funny. His love is different, and it is beyond words I cannot express, but it is wonderful.

Proverbs 22:6 says,

"Train up a child in the way he should go: and when He is old, he will not depart from it."

If it was not for the many visions God had given me, I often wondered where my children's destiny would be. Our children suffer as we do. They, too, feel the many pressures of life. Often, parents do not realize the agony we put our children through. The same way you feel your life is in a mess is the same way they feel too. God knew I needed my visions, because they kept inspiring me to live. They also gave my children hope and caused them to believe more in Him. I wanted God to know that I appreciated every gift, talent, and vision He had given me. I ran with them all because each vision served its own purpose. Know that your dreams serve a purpose, not only to give life, but to also save lives. As you begin to allow The Anointing flow through your hands, God will bring your needs forth. As I continued, my children were inspired; they saw me overcoming obstacles and achieving my goals. This inspired them to tap into their faith and go after their dreams/visions. *The Anointing Power of Your Hands* will simply connect someone else with greater hope. Allow God to work through you and He will begin to work through your children. As a parent, I wanted to train my children to believe that God is real. I wanted them to carry on in my footsteps as I taught them to fear The Lord by *simply teaching them right from the wrong*. We must let God Anoint the works of our hands to reveal to our children, as they grow up, that The Anointing is real. The best way to teach someone is to show him or her the way. Show your children The Anointing is in you. Teach them to desire The Anointing Power of God through the way you live. Children live by our lifestyles. What way are you showing your child? Whatever you are, they, too, will become, teach them impossibilities are possible.

You must know that you are a visionary. A dreamer only has dreams, but a visionary reaches their destiny. The Anointing Power of God will work in you. He wants you to put your hands to work for the vision He has given you. Desire it in your heart until God brings it forth. Put your hands to work and God will anoint them. He will give you the power and your vision shall speak for itself. Lay your hands on it and God will surge His Anointing Power through you.

Genesis 1:27 says,

"So God created man in His own image, in the image of God created he him; male and female created he them."

God has given you a perfect hand design. The majority of jobs require you to apply yourself with hands on training. Without your hands, it's almost impossible to work at an average job. So many people have what it takes to achieve the vision, but, yet, will not use what God has given them. You must allow the precious blood of The Anointing to flow through your fingertips. They will do a wonderful work and many others will notice.

Without you putting your hands on it, what good are your gifts? I know many people with beautiful voices that will sing your socks off, but they'd rather work a job paying minimum wage. Many people have God-given gifts, but they will not trust God enough to get them out of a life of poverty. They have sacrificed their future as well as their children's future because of their lack of courage. You must be prepared to show the world what you have working on the inside of you. Show them how The Power of God is working in you. Let Him perform a marvelous work as you put your hands on it. I can imagine the excitement God had as He saw the beauty of all that He created. He wanted someone to glorify His works. God created us so that He could be glorified. Let Him be glorified through you. We all notice how powerful God really is after seeing Him work mightily in another. Let the Anointing Power in your hands show the world how large God is in you.

John 20:27 says,

"Then saith he to Thomas, Reach hither thy finger, and behold my hands; and reach hither thy hand, and thrust it into my side: and be not faithless, but believing."

God has heavenly power ready to anoint the works of your hands. He loves to anoint us because He gains more glory. When you realize the power that is in God, you will know it is available to you too. He created us in His image and He created us to be all-powerful. Let Him begin to flourish His anointing power through you. Let Him grow larger in you. Put no limits on how large God will expand Himself in you. Just note, as He grows larger in you then He will be magnified through your children. I do not see God begging for anything and neither should His children. Everything that God wants is instantly done. God does not have a need, what about you? Know that The Anointing is real, and powerful things will happen once The Anointing surfaces in you. Just as our children reap from our benefits, a child of God reaps from Him. Whatever you need, God has it; if you want it, He will give it to you. In order for God to allow the Anointing Power to be accepted into your life, you must give up the things of this world and walk in God's Spirit. Remember, you can only serve one God at a time. When you really mean business and you have a vision, some things must change in your life. Get busy in your vision. God created you to be powerful, therefore, you need to indulge yourself in Him. His Anointing is purposed for us to receive power and we should show Him appreciation, daily. You have to know the One you love. After all, it is He that possesses the power to get you to your life's destiny. Without God, we would not exist. In addition, without His Anointing in my life, I would have never received the Anointing Power of my hands. I thank God for His anointing because it has brought forth many beautiful things in my life. The things God placed in my heart and the joy that He brings forth will cause one to be filled with daily happiness. Worldly things cannot compare to the peace of His serenity. I imagine that Thomas pointed out the doubts that were in his heart with his hands. You must decide if you are going to continue allowing your life to stay this way or if you are going to put forth, reach higher, and receive The Anointing. The Anointing will flow through your fingers causing you to gain a surge of the magnificent

Heavenly Power. They will work mightily through your hands.

John 20:27 says,

"Then saith he to Thomas, Reach hither thy finger, and behold my hands; and reach hither thy hand, and thrust it into my side: and be not faithless, but believing."

This man named Thomas was also known to many as "Doubting Thomas." This name followed him because of the times of doubted the truth about Jesus. Moreover, he *reached* the point of truth by touching Jesus. Thomas was one considered to always doubt until the truth was made known unto him. Though he had known of God, he was not sure about Jesus. Even being one of the twelve disciples, Thomas believed in absolutely none of his friend's own words. Thomas wanted true clarity. He was one that believed through seeing and touching for himself. No one could tell him anything. He simply had to see it to be true with his own eyes. He did not have faith. That is exactly why the generations of today are going astray; many have raised their children without knowing Jesus. Although many people know God, they say they have no faith in Jesus. They can believe that God created the world in a few days and caused Noah to build an ark, but they do not accept that JESUS rose up with all power in His hands. Jesus has all of the power. He is *The Descender.*

I know only one way that many would not take the word of a friend. It is either that you do not know them that well or you do not trust him or her. Thomas was known as The Doubter. A doubter is an unbeliever and he or she is one, which needs convincing. I concluded that he never truly knew Jesus because he did not trust that He was the Messiah. Once you know Jesus, there is no turning back. No one in his or her right frame of mind would want to be separated from Jesus because of His greatness. His love is full of compassion and once you taste His flavor, you will never let Him go. Yes, I was a doubter too before I knew Him. However, now that I know Him I could not live without Him. He has changed my life and has given it a new meaning. Life without Him is impossible to live a life of goodness. Thomas needed to touch Him for himself.

Jeremiah 29:13 says,

"And ye shall seek me, and find me, when ye shall search for me with all your heart."

Sometimes, we make life more

complicated we make life more complicated when we do not search for the truth. It is either we are simply lazy or do not want to do our own research. Often times, we just have the wrong resources. Faith grows as we decide to reach for it. We must put our priorities in order. First, Thomas needed to put His finger through the wounds of Jesus before He would believe. He wanted to know the truth for himself that Jesus was the Messiah. Many criticized Thomas for doubting. Just as people may criticize you today, do not let it stop you. He had to touch Jesus because he wanted to feel Him. Most people would have just taken their friend's advice, but not Thomas. Many people are too trusting; they will trust anyone and anything. I know there were many times people told me things, but nothing in my life changed until I touched Jesus for myself. You have to delight yourself in Him until you press yourself into His Anointing. The presence of Jesus is powerful, but His touch is more powerful. It is Anointing! Yes, I saw many things in my life and I felt His presence many times. However, when I began to reach forth and touch Him for myself, Jesus anointed me. It does not matter who you are, where you have been in life, or what you are not; He has the power to Anoint. No yoke, stronghold, or even you, can stop yourself once The Anointing comes upon you. God wants your work to be anointed. He wants it to be a powerful work and wants you to lay your hands on Him. Thomas never gave in to what they said; neither did he care what anyone thought of him.

Often times, people are quick to run with

what they hear rather than what they know. Thomas was smart; I must say He wanted to feel Jesus for himself. Thomas was prepared to do what was necessary to find the truth for himself. He did not want to trust any of the disciples. In many similar cases people will allow what they have seen or heard to stop their beliefs. Thomas was one that made sure no one was going to stop him from finding out the truth. Just because some of the other disciples were probably not what he would have expected them to be, they did not stop him from figuring out the truth. Regardless of your feelings towards another that professes the gospels, do not let it stop you. That is the key reason as to why so many visions are buried today, they allow what someone else says to destroy their dreams. I have heard so many people say, "That is why I do not go to church." All because of what someone else has done. Do not let what others do, think, or say stop you. After all, it will only ruin your life. One saying I love to say, "If someone wants to play with their life then let them but I will not play with mine."

John 20:27 says,

"Then saith he to Thomas, Reach hither thy finger, and behold my hands; and reach hither thy hand, and thrust it into my side: and be not faithless, but believing."

Thomas put his fingers through Jesus' wounds. It inspired Thomas' faith to go deep. Once he touched Jesus, He was a believer. His faith grew through the wounds of Jesus. Thomas was more than just inspired, He felt The Anointing flowing through His fingertips. Once you begin to touch Jesus as you reach forth, you will feel The Almighty presence of God move through you. God wants your hands to reach up to Him. He wants to anoint you and give you Power. The key to reaching up is that you aim high. He is The Highest of the High. He wants you to aim for the height of your life. He wants to give you all of your heart's desires, to include your major dreams.

John 20:27 says,

"Then saith he to Thomas, Reach hither thy finger, and behold my hands; and reach hither thy hand, and thrust it into my side: and be not faithless, but believing."

Often, we do not reach God in the manner He wants us to. You must look up, aim high, and feel His Anointing. Stop letting people and excuses stop you from reaching The Anointing. It is powerful! I was once in a conversation with one of my clients who stated, "It does not take all of that shouting, jumping, and stuff to praise or worship God." To some maybe not, but for me, yes it did. Once I felt Jesus for myself, I could not sit there as though I felt nothing. He is powerful and once you "really" feel The Anointing, you will never be the same. I used to go to church like I was sitting on a log and I sat on my blessings. I would hardly clap my hands or stomp my feet and my life did not change. I went to church wanting to receive, but often I did not. It wasn't until I realized that I had to become a partaker in praise, fellowship, and worship that I understood how to receive the new part of the life He had purposed for me. As they say, "When the praises go up, the blessings come down," and I needed them all. I was not a shouter or a worshiper; I was just a bench warmer. However, when that day came, I stopped sitting and I begin to praise. One day

I was no longer worried about whether or not my wig would fall off or if my heels would curl over, who cares. I went in expecting a miracle and I came out with a bigger reward. God moves as we move, and He works as we work. Eventually, I realized my praise grew stronger and so did I. My shouts grew louder and so did His voice. The Anointing is too much to sit down on; it will cause you to move. When The Anointing is on you there will be no room for doubt. You need the power of God to move in you, on you and to accomplish anything greater than you. I never forgot my first feeling of the Anointing. Immediately, I was consumed by everything within me that caused me to doubt Him. The Anointing is the most powerful presence you could ever feel, and it will soothe your soul.

His fingertip is what stirred up his faith. Because as he pushed himself towards the wounds of Jesus, he stretched forth his hands and inserted them through Jesus' wounds. He received the power of The Anointing. He felt sure with his hands that canceled out all his doubt. The pressing, the point, the tip of his fingers plunged into The Anointing. Jesus' wounds have caused many to be saved, delivered, and powered up. Finally, Thomas was able to see with his eyes and feel the precious blood of Jesus flowing through his fingertips. When you feel Jesus, you will know the purpose of His wounds. The tip of your fingers will begin to transfer the power of God in your life. I love it as I feel my way through, because the eye seeing will sometimes mislead you. God is a Spirit. We should look for Him to appear to us in a spiritual manner. You cannot see The Spirit, but you will feel Him. However, once The Anointing comes upon you there will be no sitting still. Thomas just wanted to feel the supreme presence of the Lord for himself. As he pushed his finger, Thomas was instantly delivered. The more you press, the sooner you will feel The Anointing. This press is up to how bad you desire a true heart change in your life. Your heart must feel it and you must press toward it. Your press is your reward. Know that God's rewards are everlasting; they will never die. Seek after the things of Heaven and all the power you will ever need will be right there in the palm of your hands. If you want it, then push your way through until you press your way into His Anointing. Your future is in your press and The Anointing is waiting on your push.

Chapter 8

Morning Express

*T*here comes a time in your life that you must acknowledge the truth and see the facts of life. Yes, life hurts! I can even hurt while you are trying to overcome your trials and tribulations. It is right there when the bigger challenges rise up against you, and tries to redirect your focus to disable you from going forth. It is at this moment that recognize the shift of your focus causes you to snapback and walk triumphantly toward your victory. The enemy comes again to persuade you to lose your confidence and tries to derail you from attaining your blessings. It is right there, in that place, that fear tries to sink in to torment your trust in God. This is a terrible place to be in your mind, but right there is where the true fight begins. Who's going to be more than a conqueror? The answer should always be, "Me!" But the answer seems more complicated when you are in the valley of decisions trying to find a way out, which seems impossible. Only you know within all your heart if you make another wrong decision, your life will be over for you!

Joel 3:14

"Multitudes, multitudes in the valley of decisions: for the day of the LORD is near in the valley of decisions."

Now, when you are ready to realize the facts of life, change will occur. Deciding is the most vital part of your next move because each move will soon represent a result of good or bad from the choices you made. Consideration is where you prepare for change and transformation to happen. You will either consider the facts or ignore them. I am here to inspire you that prayer changes things once you have developed the right mind set to *Make Time to Pray*. So many are too busy, and others pray, but their prayer in none effective. Prayer is something one will do on purpose because they realize life is a grand opportunity. One day, I recognized I needed to be strengthened spirituality, and adopted a heart's desire to pray. If you don't *Make Time to Pray*, it can rupture your life. Decision making is extremely necessary to cause change to happen, but you need to pray early in the morning to firmly adjust your every move. Awe, did you understand that?

Psalm 88:13

"But unto thee I have cried, O LORD; and in the morning shall my prayer prevent thee."

Morning Prayer will jump start your day and boost it with extra strength that will make you zoom. The things that were purposed to destroy you won't have any power. Morning Prayer has the power of preventing you from making terrible mistakes and irrational decisions. It also builds a fence of protection through your daily tasks. Praying early in the morning, sounds off the alarm and activates The Holy Spirit's protection of covering over you.

Psalm 105:15

"Touch not mine Anointed and do my prophet no harm. "

Psalm 5:3

"My voice shalt thou hear in the morning, O LORD; in the morning will I direct my prayer unto thee, and I will look up. "

You have renewed your insurance policy with JESUS. Often, our actions, attitudes, wrong character, speech, thoughts, and so many other things will disconnect us from our holy coverage without even knowing it. An example: many people are preaching, singing, teaching and operating in their gifts, but were fired from The Holy Spirit a long time ago because of their fowl actions and they have not yet repented. Praying helps us to transition from evil to good. We all have some good and bad in us. Situations throughout your day might cause the bad side to rise up if you don't put it under subjection. Sometimes ,you can be caught in a moment of anger and things will burst out of your mouth, such as fowl cursed words. Someone you meet or pass by can cause you to think or act wrongfully through the power of temptation. But your morning prayer will usher the Holy Spirit to help you control those thoughts and actions. We live in a world full of natural thoings and understand the natural has no conscious of good or evil, but the Spirit does. This is why it is imperative to seek Him early in the morning in order for your day t flow smoother, and be under His protection.

Psalm 102.17

"He will regard the prayer of the destitute, and not despise their prayer."

He listens to our heart beat and knows our desires. *Make Time to Pray* is the best thing you can do. It will begin to operate on your inner spirit and cleanse it thoroughly. There are times we are not conscious of our ways. What you couldn't understand when warnings came to you, then the Sprit will explain and you will be able to comprehend them.

Psalm 102:1

"(A Prayer of the afflicted, when he is overwhelmed, and poureth out his complaint before the Lord.) Hear my prayer, O LORD, and let my cry come unto thee."

At times life, it's hard to make it through when dealing with all sorts of things, people, and just stuff. If you read more of my books you will understand me more. I have been through the wringer with trying to do well. I am not saying that I am perfect, but literally speaking; if it ain't one thing then it's another. There were times I cried, but I worked while I was crying and built my faith to overcome/conquer my pain. I refused to allow that mess to overwhelm my destiny. In some cases, you cannot expect someone to rescue you, but you must, instead, depend on the power of Jesus to make your path straight. Praying will line you up in the right direction of life. When I got tired of making the wrong turns and bad decisions, I made sure I caught the morning express of prayer. It will take you through your day faster and smoother than any train on a track. Life is easier and much sweeter when you allow The Most High to take you where you have to go. Satan is afraid of our Heavenly Father, and even he must bow down or back off in His presence.

11 Chronicles 6:19

"Have respect therefore to the prayer of thy servant, and to his supplication, O LORD my God, to hearken unto thy cry, and the prayer which thy servant prayeth before thee: "

God loves and hears a repentant heart.

No matter what you are facing when you pray, before you get on your knees that thing is already taken care of. Can you imagine with all that David encountered, that the LORD Almighty was still on his side? Remember, when he faced the bear? Only one was going to make it out alive. What about when he stepped on the scene to deliver the sandwiches for the soldiers and they stood in fear of Goliath? He could not let the giant kill his family and friends. Because of his genuine love of and for God, he felt the urgency to do something, immediately. We cannot bond well with others unless we have good communication and can depend on one another. Prayer is our way to communicate with God. God speaks to us through the intercession of the Holy Spirit. It's AWESOME how God speaks to us and shows us the way. Prayer is your resolution to anything you will ever need in life; don't leave home without it.

Isaiah 54:17

"No weapon that is formed against thee shall prosper; and every tongue that shall rise against thee in judgment thou shalt condemn. This is the heritage of the servants of the LORD, and their righteousness is of me, saith the LORD. "

I love to include scripture in my daily prayer. The enemy can override your words, but cannot disable Word of God. Including scriptures is the adhesive you will need to secure your prayer transaction. It will cause a security fence to be built where nothing will have the ability to disconnect you from the truth. Jesus will be a Fence all around you because you don't need any more interruptions ripping your focus apart. You need to be focused in order to have clarity. If you cannot see where you are going, you will continue to make the wrong turns in life.

2 Chronicles 14:6

"And he built fenced cities in Judah: for the land had rest, and he had no war in those years; because the LORD had given him rest."

No weapon sets your daily alarm

de·ci·sion

də'siZHən/

noun

plural noun: **decisions**

1. a conclusion or resolution reached after consideration.

"I'll make the decision on my own"

synonyms: Resolution, conclusion, settlement, commitment, resolve, determination; More

- the action or process of deciding something or of resolving a question.

"the information was used as the basis for decision"

- a formal judgment.

"last year's Supreme Court decision"

-             the ability or tendency to make decisions quickly; decisiveness.
"she was a woman **of decision**"
synonyms: <u>Decisiveness</u>, <u>determination</u>, <u>resolution</u>,
        <u>resolve</u>, <u>firmness</u>;
        strong-mindedness, <u>purpose</u>, purposefulness
        "his order had a ring of decision"

Make Time to Pray will help you make better decisions in life so you can have rest from problems when they arise. No one should have to constantly live uncomfortable when they are protected. Once you upgrade your life by upgrading your daily protection plan through developing a better prayer life, you will be able to your enemy's tricks. It's the best you can do because it enables you to tap into the Spirit and draw strength to meet your need.

bind
bīnd/*verb*

1.

tie or fasten (something) tightly.
"floating bundles of logsn **bound together** with
ropes"
synonyms: tie (up), fasten (together), hold together,
secure make fast, attach; More

2.

cohere or cause to cohere in a single mass.
"mix the flour with the coconut and enough egg
white to bind them"

noun

1.

a problematical situation.
"he is in a political bind over the welfare issue"
synonyms: Predicament, awkward situation, difficult
situation, quandary, dilemma, plight, spot,
tight spot; More

2.

formal
a statutory constraint.
"the moral bind of the law"

Matthew 18:18
"Verily I say unto you, Whatsoever ye shall bind on earth shall be bound in heaven: and whatsoever ye shall loose on earth shall be loosed in heaven."

Matthew 16:19
"And I will give unto thee the keys of the kingdom of heaven: and whatsoever thou shalt bind on earth shall be bound in heaven: and whatsoever thou shalt loose on earth shall be loosed in heaven."

This is the reason you cannot sit there and do nothing. The longer you sit, the longer you will remain in uncomfortable situations and the tighter your situations will become. If you want to loose yourself, then get up and make the right decisions in life. It is time for you to stop resisting and become the champion God predestined you to be. You are more than a conqueror and when you Make Time to Pray, thing's in your life must change. There is absolutely no way for things to remain unchanged because The Power of The Most High is so potent that He can cause your situation to change in the blink of an eye.

Chapter 9
Keys to The Kingdom

*I*magine if you had all of the keys to open every door you needed in your life. I mean never having to wish, want, or crave for anything, but just having pure power to gain it all by reverencing your Heavenly Father because you know He is fully at work in your life.

Matthew 6:9 says,
"After this manner therefore pray ye: Our Father which art in heaven, Hallowed be thy name."

Jesus knew that God would always take care of His personal needs, as well as his spiritual needs because God was within Him. Jesus worshiped His Father from His inner soul and adored Heaven from the depths of His heart. His worship in prayer was a fervent private worship that kept Him connected to His Heavenly Power. When you open your prayers with respect and honor, and as you worship, this brings God's Spirit into you. God's Spirit will move deep in you. His Spirit will begin to caress your soul as you worship Him. Truth will arrive in your mind, as He will show you the way. As you commune with God, He will begin to change you from the inside out. Heaven will open as it fills you with His presence. Now, realizing how hollowed your Father, in Heaven, is through your worship efforts from the depths of your heart, God will begin to conduct your life and He will declare things to flee from you. The scripture possesses the first key to providing you with the method of receiving Anointing Power from Heavenly Places. Jesus knew the manner to pray which is the method for our Heavenly Father to be our life conductor. Surely, you know a conductor's duty is simply to make things perfect.

So therefore, take notice towards this manner because without True Worship we simply cannot enter into the presence of the Lord.

John 4:22 says,
"Ye worship ye know not what: we know what we worship: for salvation is of the Jews."

For many of years, many have gotten it wrong as they have prayed. Although they believe they are seeking God, truly they are seeking for material possessions. Many are worshiping God in the wrong manner, which simplifies the wrong method of prayer. God knows our needs and He has provided greatly for many of us, but often times, we worship our blessings, possessions, and things; we consider them to be miracles. God wants you to worship Him because He is The Great I Am. His name is Jehovah, which is The Most High. He is Jehovah Nissi, your banner of hope, life forevermore. God wants you to worship

Him because He has freed you from bondage, and He has taken the keys of Hell through His only begotten son.

John 4:23 says,
"But the hour cometh, and now is, when the true worshippers shall worship the Father in spirit and in truth: for the Father seeketh such to worship him."

Once you know Him in that manner, no one will have to remind you of worship because your heart will be driven with a love-passion to worship Him openly, freely, truthfully, and spiritually. Worship covers your life with His daily blessings. God is 100% Pure Spirit; His presence will cause you to walk in agreement with Him. God wants you to recognize who He is, respect, honor, and exalt Him to the fullest. Worship ushers you into The Presence of Righteousness and God begins to justify your life. True worship releases The Anointing which destroys the yokes and tears down all strongholds. It unleashes

Heavenly Power to surround your atmosphere and to walk before you. Now, as you enter into His presence through your worship, you will also enter into His Kingdom Power. Every time you worship Him in The Spirit, God justifies your life. Just as the woman with the issue of blood: her way of worship was in her press. She had her eyes fixed on her determination to touch the presence of Jesus. She no longer felt her pain and claimed her issues. It was His virtue that drew her near until she touched The Anointing. Once you begin to worship, you cannot feel anything but God moving in your life. Nothing, at this point, will stop you from moving into His presence. Your mind is not your own, your being is filled with freedom and your atmosphere is now in His presence. However, past troubles that caused issues to ruin your life will ultimately disappear. No tears of sorrow, but joy will utter out of your mouth as you praise Him. You are now at the point of no return; old things are passed away and now the newer things have been effectively promised to you. God has ushered you into His presence where no weapon formed against you will be able to prosper. You are now at the point of no return. The many things that periodically caused issues in your life will no longer trouble you; no storm will wipe you away. You are now at the point of no return. This is the most valuable key that will cause your prayers to be ultimately heard by Him. You will have supernatural praying power.

Matthew 6:10 says,
"Thy Kingdom come. Thy will be done in earth, as it is in heaven."

We acknowledge there will be a day for God's Kingdom to come again. We know the Day of Judgment is a day that will come; therefore, you want to be ready. God reigns in His Spirit, daily, in Heaven and Heaven is impossible without the presence of God. Daily, that same Spirit of God can reign in your life. When God reigns, He reigns anointing power, complete healing, full deliverance, sufficient grace, perfect mercy, happiness, beautiful joy, abundant blessings, pure faith, greater love, magnificent meekness, caring gentleness, perfect peace, inspiring hope, and so much more. The things that God reigns are not man-made but spiritually designed for those that are true to Him in prayer. God's will is performed daily in Heaven with the works of His Heavenly Power. God can provide you with that same power, today, while you are on this earth. It is vital that you believe in His Heavenly Power because all of His children's help comes from Havenly Places. You will have no worries once you know that God is in full control. Often, people tend to worry, but when you are in God's will, there is no worry. I always pray, "Father let your will be done in my life because through every will there is a sure inheritance." I want God to will to me my daily inheritance, what about you? The only way to be added to someone's will is for him or her to know your needs. They must want something greater for you to have because they have seen that you deserve it. I do not know anyone that will just will anything to anybody without knowing him or her personally or without seeing someone's effort at work. As you seek God in prayer, you, too, will notice that everything He has allowed in your life was perfectly fit for a greater purpose. In addition, everything that He will begin to do in your life is perfectly designed just for you. Allow God's will to be done in your life, for he knows what is truly best for us. God knows your needs, He knows your wants and He will give you your heart's desires. God is a perfect God and He is the Father of perfection. So, allow His will to be done in your life because He will bring you heavenly things that the enemy will have no control over.

**Matthew 6:11 says,
"Give us this day our daily bread."**

You want God to feed you what you need to be properly nourished for life. You need the Word, daily, in order to support the true factor of God. Your daily feeding isn't just for nutritional purposes, but more so for spiritual development. Within the Word of God, there is life more abundantly. Power in the Word will incorporate your life to be abundantly satisfied and victorious against the enemy. You want God to give you exactly what He knows you need. Many of times, we go and supply our own needs and never realize, until it is too late, that God did not intend for us to have it. God is a perfect provider; He is not going to give you more than you are prepared to handle. God supplies our need in perfect proportions. I need God to provide me with what He wants to provide me with on a daily basis. Matt 4:4 says, "Man cannot live by bread alone, but by every word that proceedeth out of the mouth of God." I want God to feed me daily as I hunger for more of Him because His Word is true, and His Word sets me free from the enemy. As you pray, you will want freedom, because in freedom you are able to put your hands-on things that will add greater things in your life. There is a certain spiritual feeding that you are going to need just to get to your next level. It takes time to grow spiritually, but it is up to you to earnestly invest into your prayer life. The only way to receive The Spirit is to go into The Spirit. Go after God, seek Him daily, pray to Him earnestly, and allow Him the opportunity to grow in your life. Let Him be magnified in you and through you as you endeavor to go deeper into your spiritual prayer life.

Matthew 6:12 says,
"And forgive us our debts, as we forgive our debtors."

Regardless of our daily efforts, trying to be the best believer we can, we all tend to make mistakes, knowingly, and sometimes not knowing at all. As you pray, kneel in forgiveness. When you seek God's forgiveness, you ought to have the same loving compassion in your heart to forgive others. I have seen family members that are serious church people and cannot even forgive their own brother. Still, we expect God to forgive us daily of our sins, but then we harden our hearts to people that need our forgiveness and love. I have done so many wrong things in my lifetime that I asked God for forgiveness and He forgave me. When we seek forgiveness, clears the heart and conscious of the wrongs we have committed. Forgiveness is one of the most important factors of seeking after the presence of God because it cleanses the heart of impurities that the enemy has power over. God is a forever-forgiving God and therefore, we need to have the heart of God to forgive others. Never hold a grudge because many are doing time every day on death row in prison, or even have already passed in this lifetime all because of an unforgiving heart. I would not personally want to be one trying to appear to God in seeking forgiveness and cannot forgive my own brother or sisters. Just as God has no respect of a person neither should we. Just as Jesus laid down His life for us, God expects the same daily out of His children. Moreover, just as we ask for forgiveness of God then we need to learn how to forgive others daily.

Matthew 6:13 says,
"And lead us not into temptation, but deliver us from evil: For thine is the Kingdom, and the power, and the glory, forever. Amen."

God knows us, and He knows everything about us, big or small. God knows how we are because He sees our inner secrets. Because we are born of flesh, God knows the very things that make us weak through fleshy desires (temptations). Some form of flesh is going to try to rise up; however, neither you nor I have the power to control it, but God does. You never know what is going to happen in the course of your day until it is over, regardless of what's on your agenda. The enemy knows all of our weaknesses and that is how he tempts us so much. The enemy controls temptation and he is the author of deceit, destruction, and killing. Jesus had to pray daily because He was able to acknowledge that temptation was all around Him. So, therefore, Jesus did not want to be lead into temptation and we must pray daily in the same manner; this is Jesus' method of receiving power to overcome all that is against you. Now, if Jesus walked the face of this earth with great power and authority, then we must do the same. Do you realize that if many people would have knelt down to pray for God not to lead them into temptation then they would have a second chance at life? You never know what you are going to encounter throughout your day. Therefore, prayer must be first on your list of things to do. I never leave home without praying because it is never a guarantee that I will return home. Moreover, if you notice, temptation is everywhere you go. It is on your job, around the corner, and it lives as we live daily. As long as you continue to go throughout this life without praying to the Father, you will not experience your Divine Purpose in life.

Many people, such as prisoners, people with terminal diseases, drug addicts, prostitutes, liars, cheaters, stealers, robbers, murderers, molesters, adulterers, fallen pastors, and the list goes on, could have had a better life if they had taken the time to pray in these seven key areas. It is so valuable to learn the power of prayer because the power that is in a fervent prayer warrior will get

God's attention. It will release the fullness of God to be evident in your life because the Kingdom of God will have come upon you. Prayer is the one key to everything you will ever need, and it is the greatest weapon of defense to make the enemy flee out of your life. Prayer with power is your key to a successful spiritual life, living in the anointing of God.

As you endeavor to seek power through your prayer life, the enemy will try to tempt you in every way and try to stop you from entering The Kingdom of God. The enemy does not want you in the presence of God because then he cannot be the lead in your life; that is why you have to take your prayer into worship through The Spirit. For many years I thought the enemy was so powerful with his evil forces, but the more I grew in the power of God, the more I realized that God is more powerful than the enemy. It's just like when you were a child and that bully always aggravated you, always upset and hurt you; therefore, one day you got tired of the bully and told your daddy or mother and they rushed to your aid. When that bully saw your daddy that bully got scared, ran away and never bothered you again. I believe that He [God] sits high and looks low and He will beat up any enemy that tries to mess with me. God will do the same for you. Just stay prayerful and continue growing in the power of prayer. Fold your hands, kneel down, and watch how God changes your life. No matter what comes your way, just keep praying in your faith. The more you pray, the more power you will receive from God. Although you pray, you might find yourself feeling weak or wanting to give in to temptation. Don't give up – keep praying and pray more if you have too. I have felt strong in prayer power and sometimes I felt weak in prayer power, but I never stopped praying. We cannot understand everything as we walk this earth, but whatever we need to understand God will explain it to us in the Spirit.

Prayer life is serious, and I devote my heart to God in prayer. I do not know all that He is going to require out of you, just be attentive as He begins to speak to you. I love praying because I love to hear God speak to me. He always encourages me when I need to be encouraged the most. He will give you inspiration in your weakest times and will strengthen you with the courage to continue your vision. Things have occurred in your life that sometimes tried to alter the way you serve God, even from those closest to you, but thank God for being your true Comforter. Depend on Him to lead your life because, for many years, you have done things or allowed some things to mess it up. Do not run from God any more, just fix it all in your mind from this day forward that you are going to run to Him. So now, through many life experiences, I hope you have learned to seek God's approval first and allow Him to be your guide. He has done a miraculous job in your life so far because things could be worse, but God has still blessed you. God has said, "Yes, you can!" towards all that that He has set before you to achieve/accomplish. Now all you have to do is put your hands on it. Just because somethings may have brought a halt to your work does not mean that it cannot move forward now. It is time for you to leave all the excuses, hurts, laziness, and doubts in the past because now it's time for you to move forward. God wants you to be a work in progress so He can receive the glory.

Chapter 10
Spiritual Detox

*T*his is where you connect spiritually with the Holy Spirit when you prepare to make fasting a lifestyle change. So many people do all of the other spiritual things, such as: speaking in tongues, preaching, reading the bible, quoting the scriptures, singing, praying, and so much more, but only a few fast and pray. So many people die for the lack of knowledge and many do not take the time to fast and pray. Yes, prayer works and its powerful but when one takes the time to fast and pray then it is more potent.

If you truly want a great transformation in your life, get in tune with the Holy Spirit which gives revelation in addition to enhancing your spiritual discernment. Yes, spirits are real; good and bad. Once you understand how The Holy Spirit operates, you will become more than a conqueror. Fasting and praying allows one to get more acquainted with the Holy Spirit – the Spirit of Christ Jesus. In the Spirit, you will understand how to act, speak, and build your character in being a better Kingdom Representative. The Holy Spirit will teach you things that man cannot, and, at that moment, you will be able to append the truth. I know so many people who speak of things which are not in the bible, this is why we must try the spirit by the spirit. Well, no, you cannot find it in our bible in that same manner, but you can find it here. However, how can they walk together unless they be agreed? It is impossible for two to get along if they cannot agree. It's common sense and so many are not using common sense because they are not reading the biblical scriptures in the exact same manner. There are many scriptures that can back up that old saying. While some fast, they do it for material things or when they are in need of a supernatural miracle. There is guaranteed ANOINTING POWER that is inseparable when one fasts and prays on a regular basis. Immediate PROPHESY will come forth, IMMEDIATE Deliverance happens, and Immediate Transformation occurs when one is truly connected to Jesus, the Christ, spiritually.

Fasting, also grants you the will power to sustain and to resist temptation. It is hard living well if you are in a spiritual hell. Oh yes, Hell Is Real! This is another one that people will try to convenience you is not real. Ask yourself this question, "Where does Satan lives?" Remember, he was cast out of heaven and into where? A lot of new and ancient religions try to easily persuade people that hell is not real.

In this SEASON, you will Be Held RESPONSIBLE of this CHOICE because it is a very VITAL Choice. Whoever you are allowing to speak, preach, and/or feed you spiritually is your choice. But he/she should desire for you to have spiritual growth and great outcomes for your life, especially spiritually. No more excuses! As of today, it is YOUR CHOICE.

1 Thessalonians 5:12

"And we beseech you, brethren, to know them which labour among you, and are over you in the Lord, and admonish you;"

You cannot allow just ANYONE to SPIRITUALLY SPEAK OVER YOUR LIFE and PREACH into your hearing! It could be DEADLY and TOXIC to your spirituality; so many people are walking dead today because they hooked up with the wrong people. Everyone that carries the cross is carrying it for a different purpose and they are not of Jesus, the Christ. Whatever ANOINTING & Spirituality that exists in them shall soon POSSESS you and DRESS YOUR ATMOSPHERE as it prepares your destiny. Inquire of the LORD before you connect with people. I know this exact phrase is not in the bible, but it means the same thing, "Try the Spirit By the Spirit!" If you DON'T agree, why then, are you fellow-

shipping with spirits that are not RIGHT-
EOUS?

So many people don't realize the value of connections. Connections will either feed your life
or suck it right out of you. A lot of people are
walking spiritually dead, appearing as zombies
with their faith, simply because of having the
wrong people with the wrong motives in their
life. Everyone has a motive to connect with
you, make sure you know their motives. I used
to allow any one in my life because of ministry
trying to be good to all. One day I woke up
living in hell while doing good. Yes, even in
doing good things your life can be turned up-
side down and inside out. So, therefore, I had
to recheck everyone's motives in my life. One
by one I began to access their purpose. A few

valuable questions you must ask and answer yourself:

- Why are they in your life?

  _____

  _____

  _____

  _____

  _____

- Is this a healthy relationship?

  _____

  _____

  _____

  _____

- Can this purpose cause damage to my character?

  _____

  _____

_____

_____

_____

- Can I learn from this person?

_____

_____

_____

_____

- What is the value of our relationship?

_____

_____

_____

_____

- What things do we have in common?

_____

_____

_____

_____

_____

- What purpose is this relationship?

_____

_____

_____

_____

- Is this a two-way relationship?

_____

_____

_____

_____

- Can I depend on this relationship to cause me to decline or elevate?

_____

_____

_____

_____

_____

- Did God purpose me to meet this person?

_____

_____

_____

_____

_____

- Did I ask God's permission to have this person in my life?

_____

_____

_____

_____

- Is God reaping any Glory because if this relationship?

_____

_____

_____

_____

_____

Once you are empowered with the will power to say, "No!" to Satan, your resistance will cause him to flee according to James 4:7. Make life identify your existence while you are here building your legacy.

Isaiah 65:24

"And it shall come to pass, that before they call, I will answer; and while they are yet speaking, I will hear."

Glory shall be revealed

Apostle Parice C. Parker

How does one define a powerhouse of excellence? Is this achieved by the sheer magnitude of what a survey would describe excellence is? We know that surveys are often fickle and fluctuate. And, just how do we measure the power in a powerhouse?

Did It seem a simple enough inquiry? Well, it's not, especially when it comes to the matter of Parice C. Parker: Apostle, Visionary, and One Who Simply Defies and while mystifying what a very limited survey deems appropriate. Successful Business Owner/ Entrepreneur in her 20's owning one of the most prestigious hair emporiums in the Queen City (aka Charlotte, NC) before hair matters became vogue! The author, and a prolific producer of Phenomenal

Inspirations, Publisher Extraordinaire to the masses for Christian Reality, Non - Fiction & Fiction through her enterprise - Fountain of Life Publisher's House Company. Visionary to bring that which is hidden in plain sight to the forefront.

Parice C. Parker, Apostle of the liberated and undefeated champions who dare to go beyond the limited and restrictive situations in their life to live a life of power. Parice C. Parker is a native of Charlotte NC and now resides in the Georgia area; she is a mother of three beautiful, inspiring children, grandmother, and a loving wife to Bishop L D Parker since November 18, 1992. Together, their faith has caused countless many to grasp a tighter hold on Jesus.

Apostle Parker has broken every chain when it comes to her overall health matters. Not merely a stroke survivor, a Champion of 10 Strokes, which should have killed her instantly. Her legacy of strokes led to the birthing vision of Certified Stroke Survivors and Stroke Walk. She lives because of her Faith in the Power that resides within her which has moved against dark portals of disability. She is able to move mountains with a force that is truly inspiring. She is the hope of elevation in situations where survey deems it all done and over. But, oh this is so not the case.

Visit: www.pariceparker.biz or www.thehotatl.org to find out more as to why you need to hear from her for yourself! CEO: Parice C. Parker

Phenomenal & Inspiring Books
by Parice C. Parker

1. Living Life in A Messed Up Situation
   Volume One
2. Living Life in A Messed Up Situation
   Volume Two
3. Aggravated Assault on Your Mind
4. A Precious Gift from God
5. Word Wonders
6. The Anointing Power of Your Hands
7. From Eating Crumbs to Transforming Wealth
8. The Birth of An Author Shall Be Born
9. Live Laugh Love & Be Happy
10. Power to Push You
11. Make Time to Pray
12. A Writers Heart
13. Breaking the Back of Poverty (Book)
14. Breaking the Back of Poverty Journal

Visit Our Online Book Store or Where Ever Books Are Sold

www.pariceparker.biz

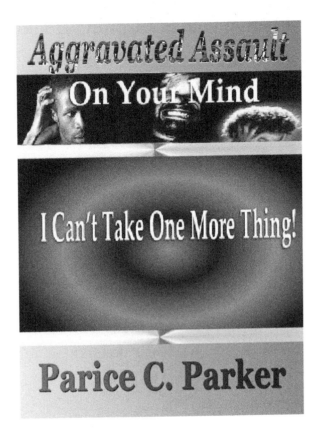

Have you ever felt, the very person you have surely loved or believed in has attacked you? It may have been your closest friend, relative, child, your spouse, or even yourself. Sometimes you wanted to cry and could not. Shortly afterwards, while gazing about the pain, tears immediately began to fall as a flowing river. Your heart has been assaulted and snared with claws of intentions to kill. A multitude of thoughts circulate in your mind and then you begin to say to yourself, **"How did I let this happen to me?"** Your situation was bound to occur because somewhere, along the way, you have allowed your circumstances to control your mind. Allegedly, you put your trust in the wrong one or thing and then you are thrown off guard. Most definitely, you wonder, "Who do I blame?" You did not realize you have entrusted so much of your heart to be assaulted through the passion of love you have given. A sense of blindness has overwhelmed your thinking ability, rearranging your life and throwing it off balance. Truly, there is an explanation and an apology due, but none is ever given. Certainly, you have tried to generate an effectual change. Perhaps, the more you have tried, the more your relationship seemed to die. **Instantly thinking, "What Is The Use?"**

Your Gift Discovery? It teaches one the value of their natural born talent and motivates one to Live Life On Purpose! This book inspires the heart, gives courage to your *"How to Ability"* and causes you to live in the pursuit of your happiness. Every natural born leader needs to read this book, it is **AWE – INSPIRING!**

God will assign the most in-depth spiritual clean-ing service through the Blood of Jesus the Christ to clean up your messed-up life. **Every messed-up situation that you are living** in will have a **Sparkling Effect** when God gets finished with you. Some things He dusts off, others He wipes down, and some need to be polished to shine. **Get**

Polished Perfect after reading this book and simply gain it all.

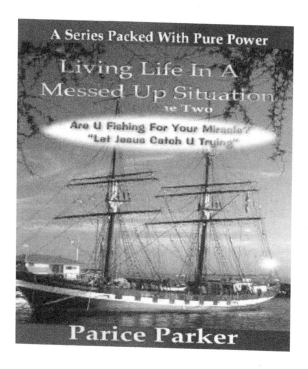

Living Life In A Messed Up Situation Volume: *Astounding* ... It seems as though many things have changed within your life, including your perseverance. Often you wanted to quit but couldn't afford to even STOP TRYING! As life twirled down so did your hope, dreams, and prosperity. Order this book today and Reel In Your Greatest CATCH! A Mega Booster is what you need, and this is it! Let JESUS catch You Trying!

The Birth of an Author Shall Be Born because there are great ideas in you. We are creators. One thing I love about authors is they have the power to form their own world to come. A sound mind contributes innovation to the world and is extremely creative. An author's concept of art has no limits. We are visionaries and see things others cannot. The power of an author is POTENT because they shape and mold through the creation of thought. Yes, an author's focus can be distracted, but what's in our view we bring forth by inventing what we see. Regardless of our circumstances, an author will let their mind take them to a whole new world and that is where the shaping begins. As we draft on paper, our hearts are led by the ink of a pen and the stroke of a key. We see doors that are shut fly wide open! We dream and then bring it to pass. An author will ride out their nightmares to see the fullness of the existence of the journey. The purpose of an author is to simply make what they see appear. Through the vision of an author we have the ability to dress our lives in expressive words just for others to visualize what we see. It is the desire in the heart that pushed the author to their destiny. Once the flame of writing grows intense in the heart of the writer its journey is complete. Authors do not compromise; they cause their dreams to come to life. Things you must know about writing a book and tips to help complete your writing journey are here. The birth of an author shall be born, is it you?

Live Love Laugh & Be Happy

It's like medicine to your bones ...

Parice Parker

Daily Devotional

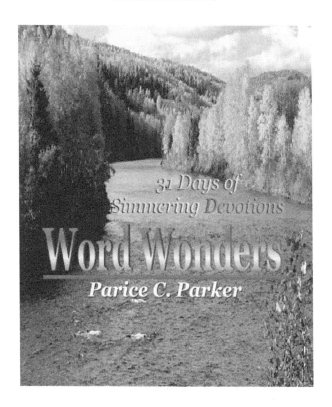

An Eye – Opening ... Word Wonder inspires your HOPE to Greatly Influence your FAITH and it's a magnificent daily devotional book to help keep you focused in word. It EMPOWERs Positive Power which causes DIVINE FAVOR to ABOUND TOWARDS YOU! Simple things you need to be equipped with more favor from on high. Get This Book TODAY!

From Eating Crumbs To Transforming Wealth

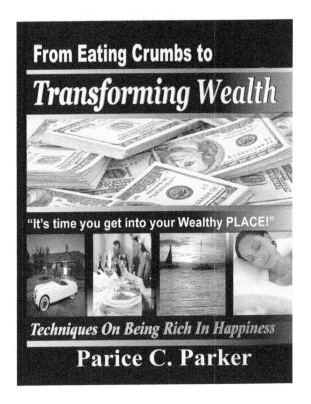

Riveting ... Finally, a book that keeps you in a thriving mental state that causes your HOPE to burst through! Now, it is time to identify the real you by introducing the TROPHY that is Hidden inside. It's your time to stop eating the crumbs of life and Indulge In Your WEALTHY Place!

Do It, Doing It! Now, It's DONE! ...
Parice C. Parker

Absorbing ... Often times you wonder why, "Why me?" Your life may not look like much right now, but keep on putting your hands to the plow of your vision and do not stop until you perfect that thing! Working a work you have never worked can be extremely complicated and very difficult, but never quit doing the work. God wants you to use what is inside of you so He can display you to the world because He Loves to be glorified! There is Anointing Power in the working of your hands because He purposely created you. Faith without works is dead, so work it!

Militant Force ...When you fix your mind on the power to excel and purpose to hit the target, then it is a done deal! Your goal now is to achieve. No one, nothing, or tiredness can stop you now. Power to Push You is missioned to cause you to be an eye specialist. Your eyes will begin to see the benefits of vision; the aspirations once accomplished, and you will have an IMPETUOUS ZEAL. No one can dream this vision as you have or push it in the manner you can, or stay as focused as you. Vision is the power to drive people, but first, one must see the fullness, must feel the passion for it to live and have an IMPETUOUS ZEAL to birth it. Vision is a life modifier and life decorator. It can give you a complete makeover from inside out. Also, when others see it, they will want to be a part of what you have. Your success will cause others to desire a much better life and give others a fresh hope to accomplish their vision. Power to Push You speaks for itself and all that connects to and reads Power to Push, you shall cause their visions to exist. It's a DYNOMITE PUSHER!

Order Powerful Books by Parice C. Parker

You can order through mail: Attention Parice C Parker P. O. Box 922612 Norcross, Georgia, 30010

Website: www.pariceparker.biz or www.thehotatl.org

Fountain of Life Publishers House

P. O. Box 922612, Norcross, GA 30010

Phone: 404.936.3989

For book orders or wholesale distribution

Website: www.pariceparker.biz

Thank You So Much!

www.pariceparker.biz

Make Time to Pray

Made in the USA
Monee, IL
08 November 2021